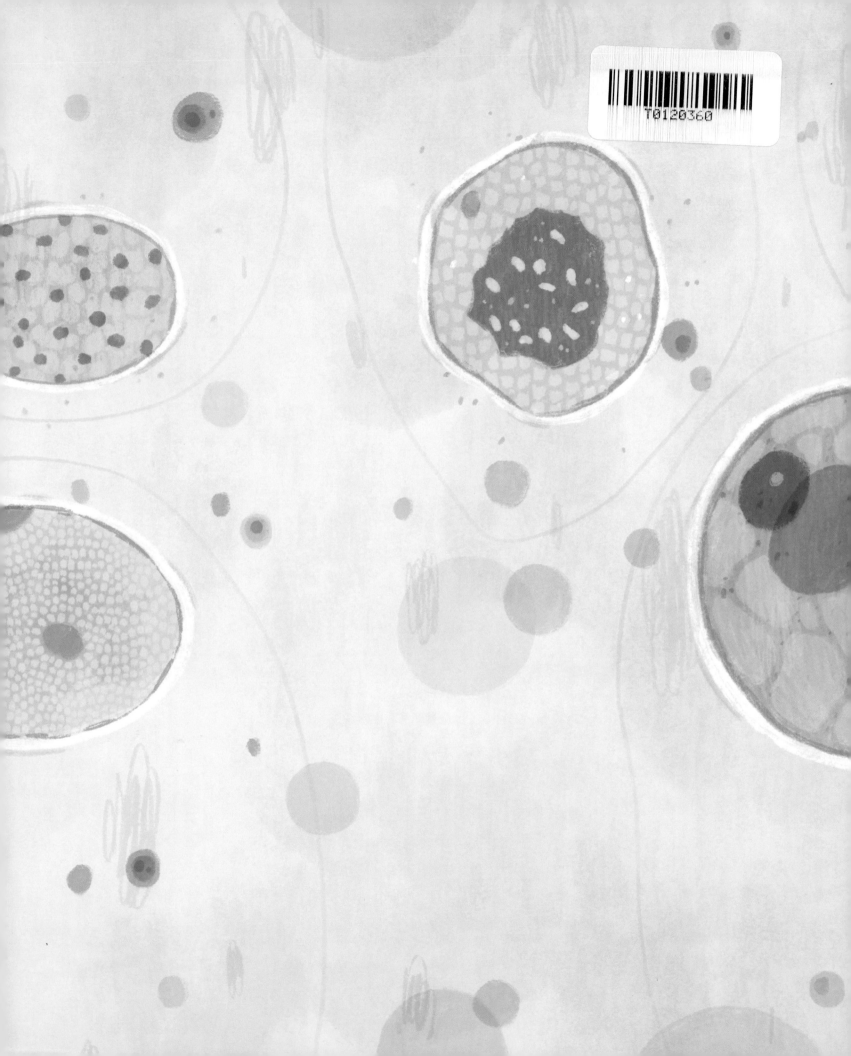

To my parents, Mel and Nelly Brown —M.M.

To Ana and Joe, my favorite scientists —L.U.

Millbrook Press
A division of Lerner Publishing Group, Inc.
241 First Avenue North
Minneapolis, MN 55401 USA

For reading levels and more information, look up this title at www.lernerbooks.com.

Photographs in back matter courtesy of Marine Biological Laboratory Archives.

Designed by Lindsey Owens.
Main body text set in Breughel Com 15/18.
Typeface provided by Linotype AG.
The illustrations in this book were created using pencil, paper, and Adobe Photoshop.

Library of Congress Cataloging-in-Publication Data

Names: Mangal, Mélina, author. | Uribe, Luisa, illustrator.
Title: The vast wonder of the world : biologist Ernest Everett Just / Mélina Mangal ; illustrated by Luisa Uribe.
Other titles: Life of scientist Ernest Everett Just
Description: Minneapolis : Millbrook Press, [2018] | Includes bibliographical references. | Description based on print version record and CIP data provided by publisher; resource not viewed.
Identifiers: LCCN 2017046995 (print) | LCCN 2017052258 (ebook) | ISBN 9781541524712 (eb pdf) | ISBN 9781512483758 (lb : alk. paper)
Subjects: LCSH: Just, Ernest Everett, 1883–1941—Juvenile literature. | African American biologists—Biography—Juvenile literature. | Biologists—United States—Biography—Juvenile literature. | African American scientists—Biography—Juvenile literature. | Scientists—United States—Biography—Juvenile literature.
Classification: LCC QH31.J83 (ebook) | LCC QH31.J83 M354 2018 (print) | DDC 570.92 [B] —dc23

LC record available at https://lccn.loc.gov/2017046995

Manufactured in the United States of America
7-53617-33181-7/6/2022

THE VAST WONDER OF THE WORLD

OF THE WORLD

BIOLOGIST
ERNEST EVERETT JUST

Mélina Mangal

Illustrated by **Luisa Uribe**

M Millbrook Press/Minneapolis

WOODS HOLE, MASSACHUSETTS, 1911

At twilight, a man lay on a dock, luring marine worms with a lantern. He scooped them out with his net and placed them in a bucket. He couldn't wait to look at them more closely.

He knew the ways of the sea, though he was not a
fisherman. His grandfather had built wharves, but
he was not a dockworker.

His name was Ernest Everett Just, and he was a scientist.

Ernest was not like other scientists.

He saw the whole, where others saw only parts. He noticed details others failed to see. On the dock at dawn, he wrote poetry.

Back in his laboratory, Ernest examined the marine worms under the microscope. He recorded and sketched their movements. "How do their tiny egg cells create new life?" he wondered. At a time when few expected a Black man to do so well, Ernest became the world authority on how life begins from an egg.

From early on, Ernest wondered about the world of water around him. Born in Charleston, South Carolina, where rivers and ocean meet, Ernest watched how fishermen netted their catch.

He learned how to read from his schoolteacher mother. After his father died when he was four, he learned how hard life could be.

To find better-paying work, Ernest's mother moved their family from the city across the river to the country. Soon after, Ernest caught typhoid fever. He survived, but he had lost his ability to read. He cried alone, struggling to relearn it all.

Then one day—a miracle! Ernest could read again. He read as often as he could, letting his imagination roam.

Words came to life as magical spirits.

Ernest attended the school his mother
created—in the town she also established.
Ernest's mother never stopped working.
Ernest never stopped observing, even
while cooking, cleaning, and watching his
younger brother and sister.

He observed how a hurricane damaged their school, how tougher segregation laws restricted African Americans, and how his mother's remarriage changed life at home. What Ernest really loved to observe, though, was nature.

Surrounded by rivers and ocean, marsh and mud, he found plenty to explore.

At thirteen, Ernest left home to attend boarding school in Orangeburg, South Carolina. It was here he published his first poem! When he graduated, Ernest returned home, hoping to begin teaching in his mother's school, but a fire had destroyed it.

Ernest left the segregated South on a steamship to continue his education up North. He dove into his new classes at a college preparatory school in New Hampshire.

While he was away, his mother fell ill with tuberculosis and died. Ernest was stunned. Full of grief and confusion, Ernest did the only thing he knew to do: return to his studies.

He went on to Dartmouth College, working to pay his own way—and to support his brother and sister back home. With less time to study, Ernest failed a class.

He thought of his family and how they depended on him. He thought of his mother's hard work and belief in education.

He had to keep going.

Ernest took a biology class and his life changed forever. In that class, he discovered the microscopic world of the cell.

Scientists knew that the cell is the smallest
building block of life, but many had only a basic
understanding of how the different parts of
the cell worked together as new life developed.
Ernest wanted to unlock this mystery.

And he did.

Ernest became a biology professor at Howard University in Washington, DC, teaching students to question and observe.

Each summer, he traveled to the Marine Biological Laboratory in Woods Hole, Massachusetts, to research and experiment.

Out on the collecting boat, Ernest looked for sea urchins, sand dollars, starfish, and marine worms. He then carefully transported them to the lab in a covered bucket so the beating sun would not damage them. Most scientists carelessly removed sea animals to study. But Ernest demonstrated that by observing living things in as natural an environment as possible, they could learn more.

Ernest also taught scientists how to thoroughly cleanse glassware and equipment for the most accurate experiments.

Using a simple light microscope, Ernest examined the egg cells of all those sea animals, night after night, day after day. While observing sand dollar eggs, Ernest noticed a wave of movement when a sperm contacted the egg. As slight as a shiver, it signaled an amazing discovery:

the egg cell directed its own development during fertilization.

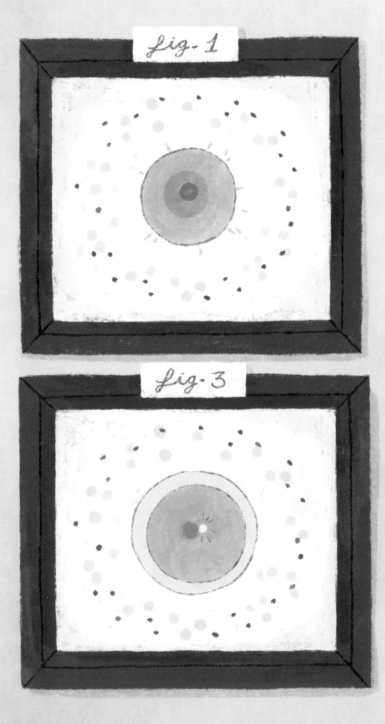

fig. 1

fig. 3

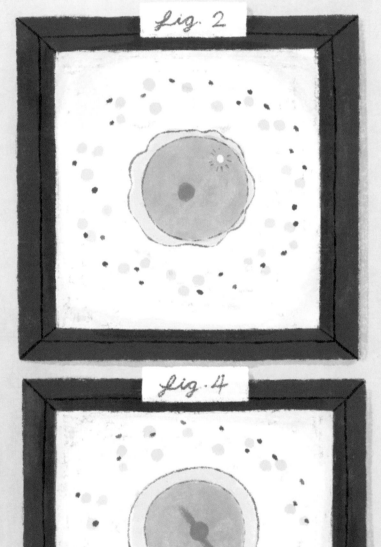

fig. 2

fig. 4

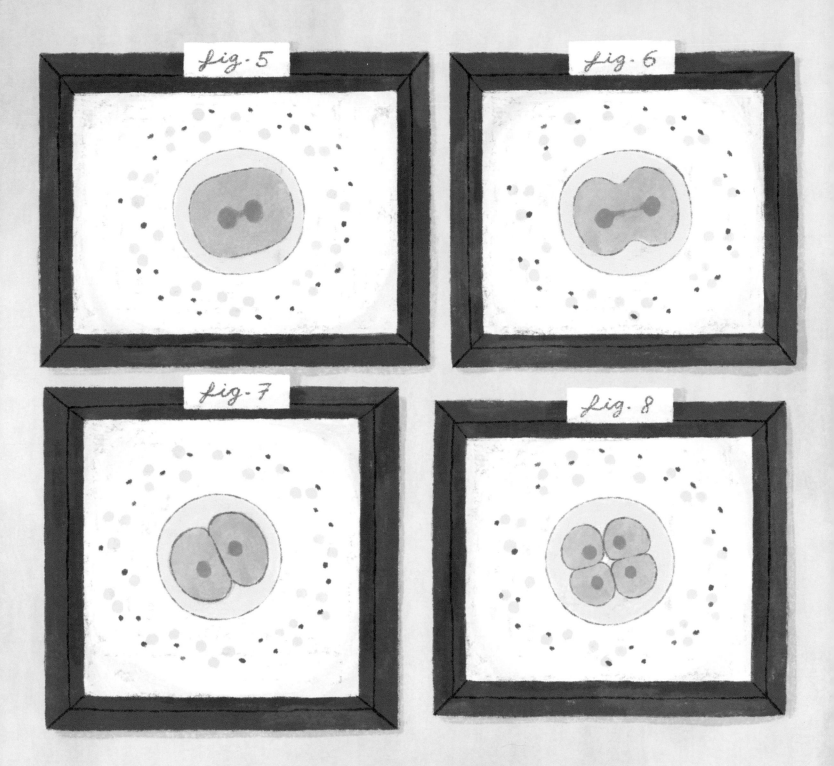

This controversial idea went against what most scientists thought at the time. It wasn't just the sperm creating changes. The cell surface and the layer right below it were just as important in generating new life.

Ernest published his research findings in many scientific papers, he traveled to conferences to share his ideas, and he won the first NAACP Spingarn Medal.

As his reputation grew, Ernest's ideas caught the attention of scientists around the world. He was the first American research scientist invited to the world-famous Kaiser Wilhelm Institute in Berlin, Germany. From then on, Ernest worked in Europe as often and as long as he could, enjoying more warmth and respect than he'd ever felt in America.

Despite his accomplishments, Ernest felt increasingly stifled in the United States. His family was not welcome with him in Massachusetts because of the color of their skin. He struggled for basic laboratory equipment at Howard. He didn't have the freedom white scientists had to choose where they worked.

The time came when Ernest refused to tolerate the segregation any longer. He decided to move to France and become an independent researcher.

Crossing the Atlantic, Ernest thought about the hundreds of students he'd introduced to science and how his fascination with cells began.

He poured those memories and feelings into his work and completed a groundbreaking book.

Through his careful observations and hard work, Ernest opened up the wonder of the universe to all of us, through a tiny egg cell.

ERNEST EVERETT JUST IN HIS OWN WORDS

"IF I CAN GIVE THE BOYS AND GIRLS A
SCIENTIFIC START, IT WILL HELP THEM IN
WHATEVER THEY MAY DO LATER."

"LIVE WITH THE TRUE, AND WHEN YOU ARE
READY TO EMBARK ON LIFE'S UNKNOWN
WATERS, PLACE YOURSELF AT THE HELM
CONFIDENT OF BUT ONE DESTINATION—SUCCESS."

"ENVIRONMENT AND ORGANISM ARE ONE;
NEITHER CAN BE SEPARATED FROM THE OTHER."

"LIFE IS NOT ONLY A STRUGGLE AGAINST THE
SURROUNDINGS FROM WHICH LIFE CAME; IT
IS ALSO A CO-OPERATION WITH THEM."

"LIFE IS EXQUISITELY A TIME-THING, LIKE MUSIC."

AUTHOR'S NOTE

Condensing Ernest Everett Just's life into a picture book was a difficult task. I found his personal life beyond the laboratory as fascinating as his scientific legacy. For example, he helped a group of Howard University faculty and student actors establish the College Dramatic Club, cofounded the Omega Psi Phi Fraternity, and presented seminars in French at the Sorbonne, a prestigious university in Paris, France.

To understand who Ernest Everett Just was and where he came from, I traveled to South Carolina. Born on August 14, 1883, in Charleston, Ernest experienced many hardships. Before he could walk, cholera, diphtheria, and tuberculosis killed Ernest's older brother, sister, a cousin, and an aunt. Ernest survived a number of natural disasters, including deadly hurricanes and the strongest earthquake to strike the southeastern United States. He also experienced a devastating series of Supreme Court decisions and state Jim Crow laws that denied Black Americans their rights and created and reinforced separate (and inferior) spaces for Black people on train cars, in schools, and in just about every other public space.

During his early teenage years at South Carolina State College (formerly known as the Colored Normal Industrial Agricultural and Mechanical College of South Carolina), Ernest's path to writing and publishing began. At the age of fifteen, a poem he wrote was published in a Washington, DC-based newspaper. And while at school in New Hampshire, he was elected editor in chief of the Kimball Union student newspaper. When Ernest was just a sophomore at Dartmouth College, he contributed to a chapter in Professor William Patten's classic biology text *The Evolution of the Vertebrates and Their Kin.*

After graduating from Dartmouth, Ernest was hired as a professor in the English Department at Howard University, a premiere institution of higher learning for African Americans. Ernest later became head of the Biology Department. He spent summers conducting research at the Marine Biological Laboratory in Woods Hole, Massachusetts. Though successful at Howard, he sought positions at other universities and institutions where he'd have better equipment and more time to work on experiments. No predominantly white American university would hire him, because he was Black—and because he was outspoken about what he believed, challenging the findings of more prominent scientists.

Ernest came to prefer working in Europe, where scientists encouraged his unique approach to biology, which included both philosophy and science. Each time he sighted the Statue of Liberty when he returned from Europe, Ernest would say, "This is where my liberty ends."

Ernest Everett Just in 1921

Ernest contributed much to science in his two books and more than seventy journal articles, some written in German, and published in the United States, Europe, and Japan. His book *Basic Methods for Experiments on Eggs of Marine Animals* instructed scientists on the proper way to handle marine invertebrates and is still in use today in an updated version. In *Biology of the Cell Surface*, Ernest explained complex scientific concepts in a way that most people, even those who were not scientists, could understand.

Ernest eventually settled in France in 1938, yet while there, he encountered new hardships. While he was working on the article "Unsolved Problems of General Biology," the German army invaded. The Nazis captured and held Ernest at a detainment camp for a short while and then released him. He fled Europe and returned to the United States. The next year, at the age of fifty-eight, he died of pancreatic cancer.

Ernest influenced many others, such as former student William Montague Cobb, the first African American to earn a PhD in physical anthropology and one of the first biomedical anthropologists, and the German scientist Johannes Holtfreter, who studied amphibian development and invented new procedures in embryology.

Ernest's scientific legacy continues to inspire through university symposia and positions, laboratory research, and institutions such as the Ernest Everett Just Middle School in Maryland, which focuses on science, technology, engineering and mathematics (STEM). I hope Ernest's story will inspire you to look more closely at the natural details of your world.

MORE ABOUT ERNEST EVERETT JUST'S SCIENCE

Basic science, or pure science, focuses on observation and experiments that add to our general knowledge. Applied science focuses on finding a solution to a specific problem, such as a cure for chicken pox. Some of Ernest's colleagues believed he should focus on applied science and training medical doctors, thinking it was a more practical career path for a Black man. But Ernest insisted on pursuing his basic science research.

Today, Ernest would be known as a developmental biologist. During his lifetime, he was known as an embryologist and also a cytologist because of his research on the egg cell and the cells of developing animal embryos. Ernest studied aquatic invertebrates of the ocean, such as sea urchins (e.g., *Arbacia punctulata*), sand dollars (e.g., *Echinarachnius parma*), and sandworms (e.g., *Platynereis megalops*), because they are relatively easy to study.

An expert in marine aquatic organisms, Ernest was also a pioneer in the field of cell biology and the fertilization of the egg. Ahead of his time, he was an early founder of "cellular holism," which combines cell biology and embryology to explore how the whole cell participates in both embryonic development and evolution. In addition, Ernest was an early ecological developmental, or eco-devo, biologist because of his belief in studying the development of animals in their natural environment.

With only a light microscope, Ernest was the first to observe two key egg cell changes during fertilization: the "wave of negativity," a wave of structural change that sweeps over the egg cell surface when sperm contacts egg, and the "fast block to polyspermy," which depends on the structural wave. These changes act to ensure that an egg cell is not fertilized by more than one sperm. Ernest observed these changes without the aid of contemporary tools such as bioluminescent tracers and high-speed photography.

In his study of parthenogenesis (activation of an egg without sperm), Ernest was the first to highlight the importance of the egg itself and its reaction to its environment. He also performed important work examining the way in which water moves into and out of cells, and he related these movements to the internal structure of the egg and the single-celled embryo as it develops. This work may have helped in the treatment of nephritis, a type of kidney disease, and edema, a disorder caused by excessive water retention. It has also helped scientists understand more about cancer. Ernest's findings influenced scientists who studied the development of amphibians and laid the groundwork for procedures such as in vitro fertilization and some of today's embryo research.

ILLUSTRATOR'S NOTE

Before I began creating the art for this book, I wanted to fill my head with everything I could about Ernest Everett Just. So I began researching.

I really enjoy this part of the creative process—investigating and learning about a historical figure—as it is a bit like time travel! I could spend hours just looking at photos, from searching for the kind of clothes people used to wear and how they styled their hair to looking at the places where they lived and worked.

Reading *The Black Apollo of Science* by Kenneth R. Manning helped me find the right people to include alongside Ernest Everett Just at key points in the book, including his mentor Frank R. Lillie, his friends and fellow scientists Franz Schrader and Sally Hughes Schrader, and his student Roger Arliner Young. Thanks to newspaper articles, I learned that two of the featured speakers at the ceremony in which Ernest received the 1915 Spingarn Medal were W. E. B. Du Bois and Charlotte Perkins Gilman, and I showed them seated in the front row.

I delved into scientific sources as well—images on chalkboards come from an 1837 sketch Charles Darwin made of an evolutionary tree as well as *A Manual of Zoology* by Richard Hertwig, one of the books Ernest used when he taught at Howard University. I also read about the flora and fauna of South Carolina and the Atlantic Coast in order to faithfully represent some of the species that live there. In addition to all the research I did at the computer, I was lucky enough to visit Charleston, South Carolina. I walked around the place where Ernest's house used to stand and was grateful for the opportunity to appreciate a bit better where he came from, even though I was seeing it from the perspective of more than one hundred years later.

After all this, when my head was full of stories and images, I began to build a clear picture of what I want to show and started putting pencil to paper. And now that I am done with the drawing and painting, I am left with all that I learned, not just about Ernest Everett Just and the circumstances of his life but about the wonder of science, research, and how even the smallest things have so much to teach us.

TIMELINE

The events in black type are those that Ernest Everett Just experienced directly. To help put his life in a larger context, some other important world events happening during his lifetime are listed in red.

Ernest Everett Just working at the Marine Biological Laboratory in 1925

1883 Ernest Everett Just is born on August 14 in Charleston, South Carolina, to Mary Mathews Cooper Just and Charles Fraser Just.

The Krakatoa volcano erupts in Indonesia, reddening the sky with volcanic ash as far away as South Carolina.

On October 15, the US Supreme Court declares the Civil Rights Act of 1875 unconstitutional.

On November 26, Sojourner Truth dies.

1884 The first telephone call between New York and Boston is made.

1885 A hurricane hits Charleston.

1886 Charleston experiences an earthquake on August 31.

1887 Ernest's father dies in June.

Ernest's grandfather dies in July.

Ernest's family begins spending winters in the phosphate mining region across the Ashley River.

Ernest gets typhoid fever.

1892 Ernest's mother quits her Charleston teaching job, and the family settles permanently across the Ashley River.

1893 Ernest's mother founds the Frederick Deming Jr. Industrial School, the first industrial school for African Americans in the area.

The Sea Island Hurricane causes catastrophic damage and more than fourteen hundred deaths.

1895 Ernest's mother establishes the town named after her, Maryville.

Frederick Douglass dies on February 20.

1896 The *Plessy v. Ferguson* ruling by the Supreme Court upholds the "separate but equal" doctrine and begins the Jim Crow era.

Ernest begins school at the Colored Normal Industrial Agricultural and Mechanical College of South Carolina (South Carolina State College) in Orangeburg, South Carolina.

1897 His mother's school (the Frederick Deming Jr. Industrial School) is destroyed by fire, and Ernest's sister is injured.

1898 Ernest's poem "The Dawning of Emancipation Day" is published in the *Colored American*, a national newspaper highlighting the accomplishments of African Americans.

1899 Ernest completes SC State College early, earning his teaching license.

1900 Ernest leaves Charleston for New York City and works for a few months in a restaurant.

He begins school at Kimball Union Academy in Meriden, New Hampshire.

1901	Ernest's mother dies.
1902	Ernest is elected editor in chief of the Kimball Union school newspaper.
1903	Ernest graduates from Kimball Union and begins attending Dartmouth College.
	The first successful airplane flight is made by the Wright brothers at Kitty Hawk, North Carolina.
1907	Ernest graduates from Dartmouth magna cum laude with a major in biology and minors in Greek and history.
	He begins teaching at Howard University in Washington, DC.
1909	Ernest establishes Howard University's College Dramatic Club.
	Ernest begins ongoing summer research at Marine Biology Laboratory in Woods Hole, Massachusetts.
1911	Ernest helps establish the first international fraternal organization on a historically Black college campus: Omega Psi Phi Fraternity.
1912	Ernest marries Ethel Highwarden.
	Ernest's first scientific article is published.
1913	His daughter Margaret is born.
	Harriet Tubman dies on March 10.
1914	World War I erupts in Europe.
1915	Ernest receives the first NAACP Spingarn Medal for the highest achievement of an American of African descent.
1916	Ernest graduates magna cum laude with a PhD in zoology and physiology from the University of Chicago.
	He speaks at the Negro Fellowship League in Chicago, founded by civil rights advocate and anti-lynching leader Ida B. Wells-Barnett.
1917	His son Highwarden is born.
1919	During the "Red Summer" race riots across the United States, dozens are killed and hundreds are injured.
1922	His daughter Maribel is born.

1929	The stock market crashes, marking the beginning of the Great Depression.
	Ernest makes his first trip to Europe for research at the Stazione Zoologica in Naples, Italy.
	He becomes the editor of *Physiological Zoology*, an official publication of the Marine Biological Laboratory at Woods Hole.
1930	Ernest is invited to conduct research at the Kaiser Wilhelm Institute in Berlin, Germany.
	He is elected to the editorial board of the *Biological Bulletin*.
	He is elected vice president of the American Society of Zoologists.
	He is the principal speaker in Padua, Italy, at the 11th International Congress of Zoologists.
1936	African American Jesse Owens wins four gold medals in the Olympic Games, held in Berlin, Germany.
1938	Ernest decides to leave the United States permanently and settle in France.
	The electron microscope is developed by Ernst Ruska.
1939	Ernest divorces his first wife, Ethel Highwarden.
	World War II begins when Germany invades Poland on September 1.
	The Biology of the Cell Surface is published.
	Ernest marries Hedwig Schnetzler in Europe.
1940	Ernest is detained by Nazis in France and then released.
	Ernest returns to Washington, DC.
	His daughter Elisabeth is born.
1941	Ernest dies of pancreatic cancer in Washington, DC.
1996	Ernest is honored on a US postage stamp.

GLOSSARY

cell: the smallest independent unit of living things

egg: a female reproductive cell; surrounded by a shell or membrane, once fertilized, it can become a new, independent being

embryonic development: transition of a fertilized egg into the basic body of the adult

evolution: the process of developing into a more complex being

fertilize: to make an egg able to grow and develop

nucleus: the main part of most cells, enclosed in a membrane, that contains the chromosomes and helps to coordinate the activities of the cell

reproduction: the process of creating new individuals of the same type

sperm: male reproductive cells

QUOTATION SOURCES

The quotations in this book are listed in the order that they appear.

"*If I can give the boys*": Mary White Ovington, *Portraits in Color* (New York: Viking, 1927), 166.

"*Live with the true*": Ernest Everett Just, "Bicentennial Moments—Ernest Everett Just, Class of 1903," Kimball Union, accessed February 11, 2018, https://www.kua.org/page/news-detail?pk=670719.

"*Environment and organism are one*": Ernest Everett Just, "Cortical Cytoplasm and Evolution," *American Naturalist* 67, no. 708 (1933): 23, available in the South Carolina State University Historical Collection and Archives.

"*Life is not only a struggle*": Ernest Everett Just, *The Biology of the Cell Surface* (Philadelphia: Blakiston's, 1939), 367. (repr., Charleston, SC: Nabu Press, 2011).

"*Life is exquisitely a time-thing*": Just, *Biology of the Cell Surface*, 2.

"*This is where my liberty ends.*": Mary Lanier Just, interview with the author, November 14, 2015.

Back cover, "*The egg cell also is*": Ernest Everett Just, *Biology of the Cell Surface*, 368.

SELECTED SOURCES CONSULTED

Researching this book was fascinating. Thanks to online databases and other resources, I was able to gain access to information that had not been available to biographers in the past. I consulted more than fifty different sources in the course of my research, and the sources listed here are those that provided details about Ernest Everett Just that had been previously unavailable. A complete bibliography of sources consulted can be found on my website at https://melinamangal.com.

Byrnes, Malcolm W. "The Genius of Ernest Everett Just." *HUGS Research Magazine*, no. 002. Accessed August 7, 2012. http://hugsresearch.org/issues/002/the-genius-of-ernest-everett-just.html.

Byrnes, Malcolm W., and William R. Eckberg. "Ernest Everett Just (1883–1941)—an Early Ecological Development Biologist." *Developmental Biology* 296 (August 2006): 1–11. Available at ScienceDirect. https://doi.org/10.1016/j.ydbio.2006.04.445.

"The Death Record." *Charleston Evening Post*. March 11, 1901. Available at GenealogyBank.

"Fire in Maryville: Deming Industrial School Buildings Consumed." *Charleston Evening Post*, November 10, 1897. Available at GenealogyBank.

"The Gale at Maryville." *Charleston News and Courier*, August 31, 1893. Available at GenealogyBank.

Just, Ernest Everett. "The Dawning of Emancipation Day." *Colored American*, 6, no. 39, December 31, 1898. Available at GenealogyBank.

Just, Mary Lanier. Personal interview with the author, November 14, 2015.

Manning, Kenneth R. *Black Apollo of Science: The Life of Ernest Everett Just*. New York: Oxford University Press, 1983.

Manning, Kenneth R. "Reflections on E.E. Just, *Black Apollo of Science*, and the Experiences of African American Scientists." *Molecular Reproduction & Development* 76 (2009): 897–902. Available at Wiley Online Library. https://doi.org/10.1002/mrd.21087.

"1900 United States Federal Census." Year, 1900; census place, Saint Andrews, Charleston, South Carolina; roll, 1521; page, 15B; enumeration district, 127; FHL microfilm, 1241521; Provo, UT: Ancestry.com, 2004.

"Sparks from the Wires." *Columbia State (SC)*, November 11, 1897. Available at GenealogyBank.

Wessel, Gary M., and Julian L. Wong. "Cell Surface Changes in the Egg at Fertilization." *Molecular Reproduction & Development* 76 (2009): 942–953. Available at Wiley Online Library. https://doi.org/10.1002/mrd.21090.

ACKNOWLEDGMENTS

I am indebted to Kenneth Manning for his meticulously researched biography *Black Apollo of Science: The Life of Ernest Everett Just* as well as his encouragement during our conversation. A warm thank-you to Ernest Just's niece Mary L. Just and grandchildren Mary Just Ader and Martinus Ader, who generously shared information, enthusiasm, and encouragement, and Wesley Jarmon, president of the Ernest Everett Just Foundation for pointing me in the right direction. Thanks to the historians and librarians who shared valuable information: Georgette Mayo at the Avery Research Center in Charleston, SC; Avery Daniels and Doris Johnson Felder of SC State University; Shawn Halifax of the Caw Caw Interpretive Center; Jody Stone and Jane Carver Fielder of Kimball Union Academy; Morgan Swan of Dartmouth; Diane Rielinger at Woods Hole Marine Biology Laboratory Library; Marianne Cawley and Molly French at Charleston County Public Library; Joellen El Bashir at Howard University; Nancy Adgent of the Rockefeller Archive Center; and to the Kathy Kinzig Eco-Education Teacher's Grant for a research grant to travel to Charleston. Thank you to Dr. Titus Reaves at MUSC for valuable information; to Dr. Gary Wessel, professor of biology at Brown University, for reviewing the final manuscript as well as art sketches for scientific accuracy; and to Dr. W. Malcolm Byrnes at Howard University for reviewing science content, sharing insights, and cheering me on. Thanks to all my friends and family who provided input, especially those who reviewed this manuscript: Nelly Brown, Stephanie Watson, Jacqueline Fletcher, Jayne Ubl, Katy Miketic, Kelly Starling Lyons, Matt Lilley, Torrie White from the Minnesota Historical Society, Carolyn Holbrook, LaDonna Redmond, Joan Maze, Mary Moore Easter, Sherrie Fernandez-Williams, Kim-Marie Walker, Buffy Smith, Lori Young-Williams, Valerie Déus, Sagirah Shadid, Piyali Dalal, Valerie, Tony, and Dominique, all my nieces and nephews, my students, Luisa Uribe for her beautiful art, and to editor extraordinaire Carol Hinz and the fabulous team at Millbrook Press. Thank you, Sameer and Mitali, for your patience and love.